Dirty, Dirty Republicans

By Gary Anderson

Contributor's Pages:

Gary Anderson (bgamall4@yahoo.com) is the contributor to Business Insider (Gary Anderson), Seeking Alpha (Gary A) and HubPages (bgamall).

Cover Page Photos:

Political figures photos taken from public domain on from Wikipedia.

Editor and Cover Design:

By Sandy Mertens (sandy@sandyspider.com)

Dedication

I dedicate this book to the citizens of the United States, who need to know why and how the Republican Party is no longer the party of great men and women, like Dwight Eisenhower.

Dirty, Dirty Republicans

Introduction

This book exposes the dirty, dirty behavior of a couple of Tea Party Republicans, Eric Cantor and Paul Ryan. These two have a special relationship with hedge funds. That relationship needs to be explored in the light of misplaced Tea Party moral demands. This relationship reveals the inner workings of the political landscape going forward. Many politicians of both parties get money from hedge funds, but this relationship is particularly nasty. For a little background, Andrew Ross Sorkin had an interesting discussion with Larry Kudlow concerning Jamie Dimon. The background of the banks in the mix is cloudy, but certainly, some bankers cannot contain their desire to roll the easy money dice once again, to the peril of the middle class. The original Ponzi housing scheme of the past decade had elements of conspiracy and premeditation, with both political parties being highly involved in the scheme. I have written about that in the book, "How to Fight NWO Economics" and in the book, "Ponzi Housing Scheme 21st Century". I recommend those books as well for more verification of the desire of banks to do bad things to Main Street. A central component to the last housing bubble were the hedge funds, which funded the shadow banks so they could make reckless loans. The housing bubble took off when those banks were able to make loans that were distributed by securitization. This book looks at the relationship of the hedge funds not only with the Tea Party elected officials, but also at how this impacts the libertarians and Ron Paul. I respect Ron Paul's honesty and desire for peace, but there are issues that need to be discussed concerning Paul, in the light of the dirty, dirty Republicans and in the light of some objectionable statements he has made with regard to the disadvantaged and the borrowers in the housing bubble. The Tea Party has roots in the Santelli Rant of February 2009 and was formed a few days later. This differs from the Tea Party rally of Ron Paul in 2007. The Tea Party leadership of Cantor and Ryan has quite different goals than those of Ron Paul. This book exposes those rolls. One wonders if Ron Paul is being used by the more sophisticated Tea Party politicians and bankers. I am inclined to believe that he is. Finally, this book takes a peak at some secrets of Michele Bachmann's funding and motives as well as my top ten reasons for never voting Republican. I have written in other books that I am no fan of the Democrats for their financial misdeeds. But the Republicans have led the onslaught of bad behavior since 2000. Certain crimes and motives by that party are being revealed at time passes, raising questions as to legitimacy of the party itself.

Andrew Ross Sorkin Just Exposed Jamie Dimon's Agenda

On Kudlow and CNBC, Andrew Ross Sorkin exposed Jamie Dimon's agenda. It is the same agenda that I have been warning that all the big bankers (sters) want. I argued that the central banks will eventually want the same thing, so that the Dimon/Bernanke feud is in house and based on a question of timing.

Sorkin revealed that Dimon wanted Dodd Frank repealed. Specifically, this is an advocacy of the repeal of the Volcker Rule. The banks want to gamble again, securitize, and guarantee all of this with government backing, or the Bernanke backstop. But it is no surprise that Dimon would repeat what Wells requested, what the IMF requested, what Bernanke ultimately wants and what the builders and the real estate industry apparently want.

We Americans as targets of all this abuse are, in essence, no better in the eyes of the banking community than the citizens of the PIIGS nations. For example, in Germany, home ownership is very low, and the German banks require 20 percent down and squeaky clean credit. However, that did not stop the German banks from victimizing the PIIGS with easy money. That caused the German banks to be the most leveraged in the world. In America, mainstreet is treated like the PIIGS, a victim of easy money. This is just disgusting. This lack of respect for mainstreet will come back one day to bite the bankers in the hind quarters.

Sorkin did let out another secret. It is essentially what I said my crocodile article about Dimon and Bernanke here. And that revelation is, that it is a question of timing. The easy money is coming, and mainstreet will be under attack again. But Sorkin implied in the Kudlow conversation that the regulation now in place is just a delay. And in the end the implication is that Bernanke and Dimon will be on the same page and will be as one on their crocodile farm. The warning is still in effect, don't touch these reptiles!

Andrew Ross Sorkin spoke of all this candidly, but unfortunately, he spoke without outrage and disdain that Dimon's antics should emblaze upon the hearts of Americans anywhere. As I have said before, Dimon and the rest don't mind artificial demand, artificial price rise, and yet, this hurts a guy with a 30 year mortgage. This makes getting a 30 year mortgage look like the most stupid financial decision on the face of the earth.

When the bankers (sters) drive up gas prices, you can just park the car. When bankers (sters) drive up food prices, you can eat hamburger instead of steak. But when the bankers (sters) drive up house prices artificially, all hell breaks loose, and people are sucked into a system that is rotten and filthy to the core.

I suggest that Sorkin has done a service, but he needs to get a conscience when it comes to this financial chicanery. It is clear that in 'Too Big to Fail' Sorkin erred in making Dimon and others look like heroes for bailing out the financial system when they set the fire in the first place and want to set another one as soon as they can.

Firefighters who set fires and put them out are not ever heroes.

Hedge Fund Cantor and Ron Paul Should Not Both Be Republicans

Katya Wachtel has a great article on BI today about the real Eric Cantor. He is a shill for the hedge funds which of course, make up the backbone of the easy money revolution. Shadow banks are backed by hedge funds and they offer you too much house with the absence of underwriting. They offered so many easy money loans that they were able to drive the price of houses up by the force of the loans themselves.

Cantor and Ryan are Tea Party candidates. Make a mental note of that. Cantor and Ryan want the rich, and therefore the hedge funds, to have even more money so that they can blow another housing bubble before 2020. This continual attack on the middle class shows the cesspool that has become the Republican Party.

Further polluting this cesspool is Representative Bachus of Alabama, **who said that the purpose of government is to serve the banks. Got that America? This is a senior member of the Republican Party!**

The Tea Party plays a function that muddles the scene, making Ron Paul look like he is schmoozing with the dregs of the political landscape. Here is how the Tea Party manifests the dirty essence of it's existence:

The Tea Party comes in and tells you that you bought too much house and it is your fault. At the same time, this Tea Party is receiving massive financing from the very people who offered

the loans in the first place! Dirty, dirty. Ron Paul, you claim to be a politician of purity. How can you schmooze with this slime? You need to get out of the Republican Party.

The Tea Party politicians, not necessarily all rank and file members, are a dirty bunch. While promoting a morality that requires you to pay your mortgages, they are getting money from the jerks that financed those mortgages in the first place!

And think about it Ron Paul. Your buddies of the hedge funds want to attack main street who were hurt by the bad lending. Oh, but that must be the part you like and what keeps you in the Republican Party. You want more wealth to go from main street to the wealthy, don't you Ron Paul! That is pretty pathetic Dr. Paul. If you don't why aren't you blasting this attempt to transfer more wealth from the 90 percent who control less wealth to the 1 percent who already control more wealth? I don't get it Dr. Paul! You must be an elitist? You certainly cannot prove you are not an elitist if you stay in the cesspool party!

I am no fan of the Democrats, because they were equally guilty of the repeal of Glass-Steagall, with the vote in the senate being 90 to 8. But at least they want to slow down the casino by the Volcker Rule, and they want to help the old and the poor. They want to protect the middle class from more sicko loans, too. You have more in common with them than you do with the Republicans, Dr. Paul. You want to slow down the casino too right? Right?

It is interesting to me that the hedge funds would want to attack the middle class so soon after the crash of the housing bubble. This seems to me to be an act of desperation. I think there should be a law that forbids pension funds from pouring money into hedge funds as is going on now. I think the hedge funds should be slapped down by the American people. These pension funds don't need more leverage and more risk.

It is interesting that the crybaby for the Fed, Steve Liesman of CNBC, was pining for the bottom 51 percent to pay taxes, because they don't do so now. Well, maybe if the Fed quit QE and quit allowing a bunch of speculation that drives up the cost of living for these 51 percent people, they could afford to pay tax. The greedy financial community cannot have it all. But it wants it all.

I have to wonder if the hedge funds and the Fed and the crony banks are headed off the cliff and want a new massive transfer of wealth from everyone else to them? Perhaps these gamblers are not so insulated and walled off from the rest of us in order to survive after all? I read where there could be 11 million houses foreclosed on. I hope people do walk away from house bubble houses, based on the moral perspective of walking away from a massive Ponzi. This could slow down these people who want to blow another bubble.

It is my contention that the powers that be want to blow another bubble are being constrained by foreclosure-gate and by people walking away. Wells Fargo wants another bubble, and wants it guaranteed by the taxpayer. I can't imagine that Ron Paul approves of all this. Why not speak out and leave the party that is most interested in this attack upon the rest of us?

Disclaimer: Walking away has moral legitimacy but I am not an attorney or financial advisor. Check with those before taking the plunge.

Wall Street Kills the US Consumer and Expects Him to Spend!

Wall Street killed the consumer but wants him to spend more. It can't work. It won't wash. We have a demand recession coming, not a supply recession. As Maria Bartiromo has been warning, there is no end demand. This is a credit/demand recession. No amount of supply side BS coming from Luskin, Kudlow, and Fiorina will do anything to help the consumer.

Here are the ways that Wall Street is killing the consumer:

1. The consumer was fooled into investing in the speculative dot com bubble. It burst and Wall Street profited while main street lost a lot of money.

2. The consumer was fooled into believing real estate always goes up by a media bought and paid for by Wall Street. The consumer lost massively, either by suffering paper losses or by actually being imprisoned in debt. Wall Street recovered, and a supply side boom among business ensued, which is artificial and not based upon **end demand**.

3. The consumer is now getting hurt by the lack of lending available, but part of that is because there is no demand for loans. And Americans don't need easy money loans, even though the Republicans are opposed to letting borrowers have information that would protect them from toxic lending! The Republicans are furious about this. They hate letting poor or lower middle class people know any more about how bad the loan is they want!

4. The consumer is getting hurt by current speculation in oil, in aluminum (thanks, Goldman Sachs!), and in food. Speculation does nothing for demand, and in fact destroys demand. Speculation is like a curse on our nation.

5. Wall Street is pushing for massive cuts in programs that give people money to spend. So after these cuts are implemented, there will probably be less spending, as unemployment insurance is not extended, as the health care cabal keeps squeezing these consumers and as house prices are not permitted to crash. Everything Wall Street is doing is defeating main street. And yet main street is end demand. It makes absolutely no sense.

It is clear to me that the *Tea Party folks, Eric Cantor foremost, are being backed by the hedge funds.* **They want a new housing bubble**. I am confident that I have shown the Republican jobs program will be a housing bubble. That is why the Republicans, or at least the hedge fund faction, want the economy brought down. It will force the Fed to act. It will force a repeal of Dodd-Frank, and actually allow massive easy money to put main street at more risk. Then when main street cannot pay the loans back they will be blamed. But let's not be fooled, because we know the process and we know who to blame, the Fed and the powers of finance. The game will likely be played before 2020. The bubble will be only for as long as Americans are unaware. Once they catch wind of it, people will fear.

People will be able to buy homes with a promise, and they will not be able to pay the loans back. Here is how bad it is. Houses are being sold in Reno, NV. for 120-180 thousand dollars, that have a replacement cost in excess of 300 Thousand Dollars! You got that people? This is happening all around the United States. It is time that main street be rescued. We need big infrastructure projects. We don't need QE but we need some mechanism to get money into the hands of everyone else besides Wall Street! It will ultimately filter through to Wall Street, as end demand picks up.

Or we can just keep going along letting Goldman Sachs warehouse aluminum in Detroit for customers, while these customers think that aluminum will go sky high. Even Coke and Pepsi are made crazy by that behavior. And we can let companies continue to bid up commodities without taking delivery of anything, and continue to weaken main street.

Yep, eventually it will cost 400 thousand dollars to insure the rebuild of a house that is worth 200k, and all because:

1. People are not paid enough to buy the house at even the discounted price and

2. The commodities used to build them keep going up.

If it weren't for a bunch of retired escapees from California and a large medical profession and lawyers up the ying yang, I don't know how houses would sell in Reno at all!

For Main Street, things are out of whack. The numbers don't add up. And Wall Street is the prime reason along with a medical profession that has a virtual monopoly on pricing. Democrats played the first bubble game, but they want, at least, some sanity with Dodd-Frank. Will they win? I doubt it.

Americans would rather overdose on the crack cocaine of Wall Street's easy money than have real wage increases with real reductions in the artificially elevated cost of living. Or perhaps they know that those wages will never materialize.

Dirty Players Exposed: Fed, Hedge Funds, Cantor

The Dodd-Frank bill has the predicted response from the dirty players in the financial system. The main dirty player is the Fed. Law.Hukuki.net has an article devoted to a really dirty guy, Fed Governor Daniel Tarullo.

This guy makes the incredible statements that:

1. All firms pose systemical risk under stress.

2. The pool, therefore, of hedge funds and mutual funds that should be on the systemic list should be a short one!

From the same website, we have the Financial Stability Oversight Council (FSOC) seeking rules that would prevent freedom of information regarding Dodd-Frank. I guess if you want another housing bubble, you need to do it in secret. That way people won't be prosecuted for starting another bubble. Investors beware! Oh, that's right, investors want all loans guaranteed by the government, with or without Fannie and Freddie. Don't worry investors, the government will have your back at taxpayer expense. Wells Fargo, the IMF and everyone important want you covered!

That could explain the fight by the Tea Party to carve room in the budget for these future bailouts. A list of FSOC members who want to keep Dodd-Frank negotiations secret is listed below.

Then, we have Eric Cantor being funded massively by hedge funds, and no doubt the lobbying effort is a massive effort to stay off the systemic risk list. We know hedge funds are funding both parties, but the push to make these Tea Party candidates toe the line is particularly odious considering that the Tea Party thinks it immoral not to pay back your underwater housing loan. And yet they are funded to victory in the 2010 election by the very hedge funds that caused your house to rise in price and then crash! Dirty politicians want another housing bubble, and Cantor is the main player!

Anyway, hedge funds that are on the systemic list won't be able to fund the SIV's that allow banks to get around capital requirements. Skirting capital requirements gives the banks a way to fund shadow bank mortgage companies that are involved in easy money housing bubbles. Therefore, the shorter the list, the more hedge funds available to blow another Federal Reserve housing bubble! The more dirty hedge funds, the bigger the easy money bubble can become!

Oh, the speculation! So much for the lie that speculation doesn't hurt mainstreet. Any banker still wanting to make that argument?

We view this website, Fierce Finance, with author Jim Kim, saying the delay in Dodd-Frank is a means to help regulators get too big to fail right. It looks to me that the delay and effort to stay off the list is a means to get too big to fail entirely wrong. For the Fierce Finance author, the delay in implementation of Dodd-Frank is a victory for the hedge funds. But I fail to see how that means it is a victory for regulators! Oh, maybe the regulators, the dirty Fed being chief, want hedge funds off the list. **A short list helps the regulators not regulate. I get it.**

Will Rogers was right. Bankers don't know much about their business. But they know all about speculation and how to make it work.

Anyway, from Wikipedia, here is the list of FSOC members who don't want too much information going out. This is a list of men and women that are most likely above the law with regard to housing bubbles:

1. Secretary of the Treasury (chairs the Council)

2. Chairman of the Federal Reserve

3. Comptroller of the Currency

4. Director of the Bureau of Consumer Financial Protection

5. Chairperson of the U.S. Securities and Exchange Commission

6. Chairperson of the Federal Deposit Insurance Corporation

7. Chairperson of the Commodity Futures Trading Commission

8. Director of the Federal Housing Finance Agency

9. The Chairman of the National Credit Union Administration Board

10. An independent member (with insurance expertise), appointed by the President, with the advice and consent of the Senate, for a term of 6 years.

Paul Ryan Budgeted In a Massive Ponzi Housing Boom
To Save His 6 Trillion

We all have heard what is happening in England, as austerity is causing more pain and less consumer spending. We know what happened in 1937, as the United States introduced austerity and started the depression all over again. Now we find out that Congressman Ryan is counting on a gimmick to save the 6 trillion dollars he boasts about. From Marketwatch is an article that exposes the little scam, though short in details. What we know is that Ryan is predicting massive excess inventory being built going forward in order to reach his goals.

While there is skepticism that this boom will take place, the powers that be would certainly want it to take place. Without something, they obviously know that the cuts will tank the US economy. Yes, predatory banking is here to stay. There are some signals that this is what the central banks want. First, Bachus of Alabama, as I have said, wants to do away with the Volcker Rule. This would allow the shadow banking system, funded by hedge funds, to rear its ugly head unimpeded.

Certainly, I have been writing about how Bernanke wanted the backstop of government guarantee for loans, and with this moral hazard in place, banks would have little constraint upon their reckless lending. The reintroduction of predatory lending, now that we see Ryan's budget scam unveiled, no doubt assumes that people will take the same risks that they did in the last housing bubble. Only this time they will be fully aware of the outcome. Fear will likely grip these markets much more quickly, and Americans will be less inclined to be trapped with unsustainable paper profits.

I wrote recently that once the TBTF banks experienced the crack high of securitization, that they will want the fix again. Ryan is assuming they will get that injection from the Bernank.

So, Ryan, being an apparent foot soldier of the central bank cartel, is for starting the credit crisis all over again. What a guy! With patriots like this we really don't need enemies do we?

I would say to investors, be very careful. But wait, all these loans will be guaranteed. Joe Taxpayer will be the backstop. No need to be careful. Ride that wave of moral hazard. As for Paul Ryan, the clown is hoping that this phony housing bubble will drop the unemployment rate to 2.8 percent. Happy days will be here again. But don't let your babies grow up to be homeowners unless you want them to be crushed by debt like the last wave of unsuspecting victims.

For further study read:

http://blogs.marketwatch.com/election/2011/04/14/the-ryans-plan-mysterious-house-boom/

http://macroadvisers.blogspot.com/2011/04/economic-effects-of-ryan-plan-assuming.html

Top 10 Reasons Why Ron Paul Should Be a Democrat!

There are many compelling reasons why Ron Paul should become a Democrat or an Independent caucusing with the Democrats. I will try to list some really good reasons here:

1. He could team with Bernie Sanders I-VT, another individual who hates the behavior of the Fed. Bernie Sanders wants the Fed audited just like Ron Paul does. Bernie Sanders has written extensively on the crony capitalism of the Federal Reserve Bank.

2. The Republicans have gotten just too corrupt. Washington DC is corrupt but the Republican Tea Party guys, Cantor and Ryan, were quietly funded to the tune of 10 million dollars in the 2010 mid term election by the hedge funds. A lot of this money was funneled to the Tea Party and other Republicans through third parties according to an MSNBC article. This is particularly odious because this same Tea Party says it is immoral to walk away from your home loan. Yet the same Tea Party is being funded by hedge funds that funded SIVs with credit and which allowed much of the housing credit crisis to build up and then crash. Couple this with the off balance sheet nature of the SIVs, and you had shadow bank weakness even advance to the doors of major commercial banks. The toxic loans were made possible by the funding from the hedge funds.

3. The hedge funds want to take over the political system yet again. So, why would hedge funds try to take over the political process with Cantor in the lead? Look at reason number 9 for one thing. And apparently Cantor is the point man for hedge funds. And it is not just taxation of hedge fund profits that are the cause of this new push with the Tea Party. It is also because hedge funds hate the Dodd Frank regulations. They want the capacity to blow more bubbles and that is difficult in the current atmosphere. Americans should rejoice that their gas is not at 5 bucks a gallon because that is how the hedge funds profit. They profited off the housing bubble as wealth was transferred to them from the middle class. The shadow banking system was massive compared to the regular regulated banking system. The SIVS that sunk Enron and others were also used to pump up and then sink the housing sector. There is no room in the Republican Party for a guy like Ron Paul who hates this corporatism.

4. Ron Paul cannot separate himself from the Tea Party in the thoughts of the man on the street. Many people believe that Ron Paul founded the Tea Party. He did not, because it was founded on February 22, 2009 by people in Chicago and St. Louis. But he is known as a spiritual father of the Tea Party. He cannot seriously think to unwind that connection to people who now are getting the bulk of hedge fund favors without leaving the Republican Party. Remember when Hennessy was hanging around the Kudlow show and Kudlow was calling him the father of the Tea Party? He was there in February, 2009.

5. Some libertarians believe in a social safety net. There is room for libertarians to be Democrats in these extreme times. It is necessary that main street be protected from Wall Street and their very destructive hedge funds. Chris Dierkes says that the social safety nets are implied in Adam Smith's views regarding the limitations of markets and in the morality of a civilized society not totally given over to

market greed. The article was written in 2009 when indeed, the Democrats were benefiting from hedge fund donations and from the corruption of Geithner's refusal to prosecute the bankers who did wrong (which would have included himself?) But now the tide has turned and the Republicans are the beneficiary of the bulk of hedge fund corruption.

6. We have to put a thumb on the Fed rather than destroy the Fed. If we nationalized the Fed then 1.6 trillion dollars owed to the Fed could simply be washed away. The result of banning the Fed would be catastrophic. We would have short term loans with balloon payments, forcing borrowers to become the gamblers. I reject the idea of those loans as much as I reject the idea of easy money loans from the shadow banks. Ron Paul should seek stability in the 30 year fixed mortgage. It worked for decades. It didn't cause bubbles. It was based on responsible underwriting. How can we get back to the sound 30 year fixed mortgage with 20 percent down? We can't get there if the Republican corruption and hedge fund power consolidates. Ron Paul needs to totally repudiate the easy money cabal. Nationalization of the Fed and a law banning easy money loans to all but the upper rich is needed. The libertarians are always talking about savings and investment. The only way to affirm savings and investment is to repudiate the casino of easy money lending and securitization! Libertarianism cannot, in its present form, control the monster.

7. Spencer Bachus of Alabama said in late 2010 that the purpose of government was to serve the banks. How can anyone stay in a party that spews that kind of filth? That is un-American. Yes, Dodd-Frank needs more teeth, but that can be done. It needs to be able to wind down bad banks. Ron Paul can't be against a stronger Dodd-Frank can he? Bachus opposes Dodd-Frank because he wants the regulators to serve the banks, not the other way around! Surely Ron Paul can't swallow that line of BS can he?

8. Ron Paul needs to realize that the traditional party of the people are the Democrats and the traditional party of the banks are the Republicans. To the extent that this can be restrengthened in our time is the extent to which the American people will have a fighting chance. No one is saying that Ron Paul and Bernie Sanders will see eye to eye on many things. Sanders wants nationalization of oil. Ron Paul is from an oil state. But working together they could help stop speculation, which is a major reason why oil prices continue to gouge Americans daily. Again, if Ron Paul is for savings and investment as a means to build the American dream, he cannot be for credit and speculation, the hedge fund way, can he?

9. The most important part of Dodd-Frank is that there are many systemically risky companies, including many hedge funds, that are no longer able to play with the financial system's stability. This gripes the hedge funds to no end. They can't play anymore. And they don't like it. Small startup companies rely on a smaller shadow banking system as we see in the Time Magazine article dated June 27, 2011. This article, titled Is Dodd-Frank Reviving the Shadow Banks seems written to give the hedge funds the ability to hit Dodd-Frank. Ron Paul, the hedge funds are being contained and they don't like it. They want to play and risk all but now they cannot play. The Democrats are stopping their entrance into the casino. And this affects their shadow activity in house lending as well. Do you really want this monster touching the major

banking system that could cause a systemic meltdown? Wouldn't it be better to caucus as a Democrat to stop these massive hedge funds from playing the shadow banking game?

10. The Democrats appear to be the party of compromise, while the Republicans stress out the nation with their refusal to be political. Sometimes you can't always get what you want. Ron Paul never gets what he wants so maybe he could be a more effective leader if he learned to compromise. Do we want the financial system to operate as a casino or as a responsible organism? This is what joining the Democrats would be all about, Ron Paul, compromise. I support the ban of certain speculation, like in housing and foodstuffs. And oil speculation should be looked at as well. If Ron Paul sees the merits of controlling a market for the greater benefit of civilization, perhaps he could see himself as a Democrat.

Eric Cantor Just Lied.
Buffett Said He Wants His Taxes Raised!

Eric Cantor is starting to tin foil this whole budget debate. He just mentioned that people don't ask for their taxes to be raised. However, we know that Buffett/Munger of Berkshire Hathaway have both said that their taxes need to be raised. I don't think this Cantor guy is the sharpest tool in the shed. I think his political sense rivals Congressman Ryan who was assigned to the bleachers after trying to take away Medicare.

Cantor has said that it should be against the law for relief emergency aid to disaster victims without making equivalent cuts in the budget elsewhere. In other words this guy is a madman. Where does the Tea Party get these guys? Ryan wants another housing bubble, and Cantor wants one too, by the way he pushes for tax protections for the rich.

Indeed that is what this is all about. The plan to tax the rich does not come with a cushy job at someplace like UBS (think Phil Gramm after the repeal of Glass-Steagall). I don't think that Ryan has a clue that his obvious ambition is over the top, or should I say, over the cliff. The central bank wants a bubble at some point. But even Bernanke is not ready yet. Cantor is front running the central banker!

Cantor's profanity laced video in 2009 demeaning union workers is a hateful thing. His desire to create a bubble based on the rich having too much money, with which they will churn up prices in commodities, is not patriotic. America cannot stand these easy money attacks, that seem to come with ever more frequency.

Here is my solution to the Cantors of the world:

1. Stop using the products of the banks. Boycott all real estate loans.

2. Support anyone who has the desire to build a jobs program. We have Hoover in Obama and we have worse in Cantor. We are so far right that the economy is in jeopardy. I would rather have an end to QE and a real jobs program. While military spending causes few dollars to turn over, domestic jobs spending would immediately be turned over in the community. It would be better than the QE3 that will blow oil prices beyond the tolerable.

The Republicans want inflation. I know Peter Schiff cannot see this but it is true. Easy money is inflation and the Republicans are drooling for more easy money. Schiff knows what easy money can do as he predicted the housing bubble! But he can't see that his Republican buddies want easy money lending inflation? Hmmm.

Cantor divides the young from the old, a typical central bank ploy. He warns young people to not rely on pensions they may earn, and I suppose he even is talking about 401k's since most companies are going to that pay system. What is his point?

He wants less regulation, which means he wants the casino banks to be free to lever up to their eyeballs. Debt is good if the banks can make money on it. That is Cantor in a nutshell.

If I thought for a moment that Cantor was against the banks and for the people, I would support him. But the truth is he postures being against the banks, but really he isn't. He did not oppose Ryan's massive tax breaks for the banks. His wife works for a bank that was bailed out by TARP! I didn't hear him complain, did you?

And remember Cantor's plan for banks to insure their mortgages? Turns out the taxpayer would have been on the hook for most of the mortgages anyway. Thanks for nothing Eric. Don't tell us you are for the taxpayer until you free us from mortgage guarantees and securitization. You sound like a central banker more and more Eric.

The IMF War on Mainstreet: Housing Bubble by 2020 and More Fees

The game plan is pretty clear. If you go to this Portuguese website, Algarveresident.com, you see that the VAT tax is at an all time high. The VAT tax is an IMF tax. It is a hidden tax. While the IMF wants VAT taxes, it wants austerity, using it's Enforcers, S & P, Moodys and Fitch to do the dirty work. I can't prove that the ratings agencies are the foot soldiers of the IMF, but that relationship should be watched carefully. Taxation throughout the world will be hidden like VAT, and will creep up on main street, like the middle tax cut ending in January 2012, and like the tolls that will increase throughout the world, all to protect the fortunes of the Uber Rich and to raise taxes without looking like you are raising taxes.

Then the IMF wants to blow another housing bubble and collect more money for the bankers that way. And all the while the IMF chastises the banks for irresponsible lending, on it's website.

Well, I don't buy it. One gets the idea that the IMF wants austerity to protect bond investors. But I think the IMF wants austerity to destroy our stock market and increase world debt as mentioned at Davos this year. In fact, from this deflationary position, as I have argued before, the IMF is able to establish securitization guaranteed by government. If the IMF were concerned about government's getting out of debt, then why would the organization insist on a future guarantee of all loans, including odious easy money loans that can only destroy the balance sheet of government? This is a replacement of debt to help main street with a debt to help banks once the next ponzi fails.

Why do Fannie and Freddie now own 1/2 of distressed homes? Most of those loans were not originally guaranteed by Fannie and Freddie! Fannie and Freddie took on a lot of loans that were not guaranteed. A lot of the theft by the banks that is still going on has to do with these loans that were not guaranteed, as the private mbs assault juiced the housing bubble to dangerous heights.

You cannot trust the IMF/BIS/Ratings Agency alliance. The alliance may not be formalized, but these do work toward the same ends. It is an unholy alliance and it is more about carving out a place for government to cover the bad bets of banks with certain guarantees. And it does not matter if Fannie or Freddie exist or not, the guarantees will be absolute. All of the following seek guarantees for most of the loans made in real estate or they want the 30 year fixed mortgage, that never blew a single bubble, to go away. To me this is just a smokescreen to revive easy money securitization because the banks want the crack high of securitization. This isn't really about the 30 year fixed! They can't make big money with a 30 year fixed! The list of IMF co-conspirators is large:

1. Jamie Dimon

2. Wells Fargo

3. Realtors (While the article accurately speaks of private mbs lending, the threat to the 30 year mortgage is made in this article.)

4. Home Builders

5. Paul Ryan

6. Eric Cantor

7. Federal Reserve

8. Citigroup

9. Anyone else who hates Dodd-Frank

10. Anyone who can circumvent Dodd-Frank while pretending the law is in force.

11. IMF

It is really sickening how our government refuses to protect us from odious loans. I believe that the US should pay debts to creditors, such as the Chinese, the Japanese, US citizens and the Russians. I don't think that the US is obligated to pay for easy money mistakes. It is an odious debt upon the nation. The next housing bubble attack on main street will likely occur before 2020. That, along with more fees as taxes, will allow more money to funnel to the Uber Rich while the burden of taxation will increase to those very people being offered the toxic easy money loans!

The wealthy want toll roads here just like in Portugal. The G20 allowed the United States and first world countries to be controlled by the IMF and it is for the purpose of raping main street again and again. We are now no different than the emerging countries that have been raped by these parasites. We need to know that right and left commenters have concerns about this new power play threat to the developed nations.

We are, people, in a war that is being waged against us by an enemy we did not choose nor do we wish to fight. But we can't lay down either. We need to shame the IMF and these bankers and make that shame stick like a scarlet letter.

Article Links:

http://www.businessinsider.com/imf-wants-implicit-guarantees-for-loans-just-like-wells-fargo-2011-2

http://www.algarveresident.com/42070-0/algarve/in-my-view-moodys-the-imf-and-odious-debt

http://www.housingwire.com/2011/03/25/wells-fargo-study-finds-new-kind-of-homebuyer-on-the-way-millennials

http://www.businessinsider.com/andrew-rice-sorkin-just-exposed-jamie-dimons-agenda-2011-6

http://www.businessinsider.com/i-was-right-ryan-has-to-have-a-ponzi-housing-boom-to-save-6-trillion-2011-4

http://www.businessinsider.com/wells-fargo-bank-leads-securitization-attack-on-unsuspecting-taxpayers-2011-2

http://www.algarveresident.com/0-42774/algarve/Portuguese-tax-rates-for-vat-and-irs-hit-record-highs

http://www.businessinsider.com/dimon-versus-bernanke-all-is-not-well-at-the-crocodile-farm-2011-6

http://voicesofrealestate.blogs.realtor.org/2011/02/18/why-we-value-the-government%E2%80%99s-role-in-housing-posted-by-ron

http://www.europeansecuritisation.com/Market_Standard/121208-Securitized%20Products-Restart%20Securitization.pdf

http://www.lambslain.com/2011/07/private-operators-are-taking-over-roads.html

http://www.businessinsider.com/hedge-fund-cantor-and-ron-paul-should-not-both-be-republicans-2011-7

http://www.businessinsider.com/imf-wants-implicit-guarantees-for-loans-just-like-wells-fargo-2011-2 http://www.businessinsider.com/biggest-middle-class-tax-increase-in-history-will-come-in-five-months-2011-8

For Further Study:

http://allafrica.com/stories/201108120277.html

Are Republicans Agents of the IMF? Look at Italy!

The Republicans have become the agents of the IMF bank! We know that the Democrats are not guiltless, with Obama wanting the IMF inspired VAT tax early in office. But it is the Republicans who want the balanced budget in the US, similar to what is being imposed upon Italy. It is pretty disgusting if you think about the reasons why this push for austerity is so pronounced.

The Italian balanced budget is being forced upon the nation in exchange for liquidity. Certainly, the Republicans almost got a balanced budget amendment through the debt ceiling debate. While it is the Euro zone and ECB that are applying the screws to Italy, the IMF has called for these reforms on their website for a long time, along with the Italian government selling lots of public property. Sound familiar? The IMF is deeply involved in this austerity push worldwide, as we have seen elsewhere.

The thing that makes all this so odious and unacceptable is that the IMF is at the forefront of seeking massive securitization of housing loans, government guarantees of such loans, and another housing bubble. The IMF is the enemy of main street because bankers are the enemy of stable real estate prices. A balanced budget just so that housing bubbles and guarantees can be established is too much for citizens to bear. It is wrong and it is at the root of speculation on shelter, a basic human need.

So Republicans have become the central agents of bank greed. I think people concerned about their retirement futures should avoid voting for this foreign agent, the Republican Party. I have written that both Eric Cantor and Paul Ryan are agents of the hedge funds, seeking to keep as many off the list of systemic risk as possible. The more hedge funds free of the label means the more hedge funds that can funnel money to shadow banks making easy money real estate loans.

Even if you have a 30 year fixed, which is normally a prudent loan, that loan is put into jeopardy because of the easy money loans to your neighbors, which can introduce artificial demand and price. Your 30-year loan can be a losing proposition if your house crashes in value through no fault of your own due to this artificial easy money demand. As long as easy money is an option, you may be better off renting and investing the rest.

The IMF plan is pretty clear, and that is to extend the casino on a more regular basis to main street. The casino of easy money home loans can be manifested every decade if these people get their way. Certainly, our big banks want these loans, and I have written about Wells, Bernanke, Dimon and others wanting guarantees and easy money. The guarantees actually help the easy money as investors view the bonds from these loans as being virtually risk free. But cheap money does not last forever, and these guarantees could come home to roost. Can you imagine the cuts needed by government when every last mortgage is guaranteed in a housing crash?

If Americans are serious about keeping the social safety net, and the safety of stable housing prices, they need to rise up against the IMF and the guarantee of easy money loans. Just remember that when the Republicans say that government spending crowds out investment, what they really mean is that government spending crowds out government guarantees of loans.

Of course, in Italy, house prices did not crash in the recession. So who knows what the bankers have cooked up for the Italian housing economy. However, one thing is sure, in the US, the banks want the capacity to lend to a market that is increasing in value. The banks fear the lack of demand without a housing bubble based on easy money. The banks no longer want the 30 year fixed. And that is bad for America, but these agents of the IMF, the Republicans, are blind to that fact.

People seek securitization of loans in order to pawn risk onto others. That is what banks want to do. The only way they can convince the investors that the risk is low is through guarantees of loans by government. And that is where the balanced budget amendment and the Republican IMF operatives come in. Don't vote for them and boycott the 30 year mortgage. Bankers were trusted from after the depression until about 1995. That absence of trust in bankers is now permanent without a constitutional ban on easy money to all but the wealthiest Americans.

Early this year, investors were allowed an extension of the no flip rule. So going into the second year, foreclosures are being gobbled up by investors in an effort to rekindle the housing market. If that manipulation is being allowed, look to possible intervention by the central bank in purchasing homes. We know that the Fed buys commercial real estate, so that it would be a sign of easy money if they go into the residential market. Artificial price rise is only sustainable by easy money as a help.

Cantor and the Republican operatives of the IMF must be thrilled.

Larry Kudlow:

Your Spin Was Bad. Wall Street: Demand Is Dead

I thought, Larry, that your performance in making a plea for social security money for a hungry Wall Street was your worst performance. Then I thought your performance in stating that class warfare came from the bottom instead of the top was your most shameful performance. But today, your spin against Obama, admittedly the Hoover of our time, was the most disgusting.

It went down like this:

The S & P wanted tax revenue to balance out cuts. I listened to the interview over the weekend. But we know that when Obama spoke today about wanting the new taxes, the stock market tanked. How convenient Larry Kudlow. We know the spin. Cut even more out of main street and give Wall Street more tax cuts? The spin is on, being paid for by the hedge funds. Cantor, the biggest recipient of hedge fund money must be thrilled.

My point is, the class war on the middle class is continuing. The stock market can actually tell the president what to do because the market went down decidedly, after he stopped speaking. We know it was the hedge funds, Larry, because it was programmed, electronic trading. It was all by machine. It could have been high frequency. Even Cramer said you had to get out of the way of the machine.

I noticed that the mainstream press had very little on the real S & P call for more taxes. How convenient Larry. Just right up your alley of disinformation.

All we have had is stimulus for Wall Street. How can anyone expect main street to back Wall Street up with consumer spending when all the stimulus, except state help and unemployment insurance, has gone to Wall Street?

We need jobs programs, infrastructure programs, and everything that Charlie Gasparino, some say banished from CNBC to Fox Biz News, hates. Those programs create end demand. Perhaps the banks fear because if we are bailing out the real economy, there won't be any money left for the banks. The mosquitoes of the banks, the hedge funds, will run out of blood. How scary!

But Obama needs to quit being Hoover. And the reason is, the Republicans will have no FDR waiting in the wings. The Republicans have a bunch of wacko, weirdoes waiting in the wings.

The conspiracy theorist in me wonders about the connection of S & P to the IMF. I don't trust or like the IMF. The IMF wants a rekindling of securitization of lending, with a government backstop. I just wonder how much influence the **IMF has on Standard and Poor's. Does S & P stand at attention if the IMF barks?**

The conspiracy theorist in me also wonders about if all this market dislocation is a temper tantrum against Dodd-Frank. This recession is totally based on lack of demand. So the banks and hedge funds are thinking that we need more easy money toxic loans in order to create demand! The hedge funds are panicking?

But whatever happens near term, consumers need more money. I would like to see Americans park the car until oil gets down to around 50 bucks.

Maybe we could have a consumer slogan on the price of oil that goes like this:

I Can't Drive Until Oil Hits $55! And set it to the music of Sammy Hagar!

That should rattle the oil markets. (I can dream.)

But what I am wondering about is **how the hedge funds can have it both ways?** They want end demand on main street. But they also want more stimulus for themselves. It should be pointed out that in a deflationary world, you can't pay US citizens more. Their only raise will come by a stronger dollar or easy money loans. The Street cannot tolerate the stronger dollar. But, the consumer cannot tolerate the easy money loans.

Something has to give!

Michele Bachmann's Wall Street Connection:
The Club for Growth

Michele Bachman is connected to Wall Street through Steve Moore's Club for Growth.

The club was founded in 1999 by Steve Moore, frequent guest of Larry Kudlow and a member of the Wall Street Journal's editorial board.

Steve is a pretty nice guy. But the Club for Growth is anything but nice. The club has a PAC, and supports very conservative politicians, including Bachmann.

The Club for Growth supports supply side economics, which Herbert Hoover called "percolation" and Art Laffer called "trickle down". Of course we have little demand in society so theoretically you could supply all the loans you want and no one would want them or qualify for them.

However, modern supply side economists, and Bachmann, will have a diabolical success if the key variable, credit scores, are loosened as a means for determining loan recipients. If you literally give money away to any warm bodies, you will have people borrow, and you will generate bubbles.

The only problem with this is that it undermines the stability of house prices and undermines the 30 year fixed loan. Your house could crash in price by the time your stable loan matures, with all the easy money that the Club for Growth apparently wants to flow. It becomes problematic to take out a fixed 30 year loan, the anchor of American greatness in property value, if your house value is subject to so much manipulation going forward.

Barney Frank was a part of the original housing bubble, kick starting it with the CRA. That bubble was then taken over by the shadow banks and investment banks, and became much larger between mid 2003 until the crash than it would otherwise have been have been. However, with Dodd-Frank, Barney has taken the traditional Democratic view that main street must be protected from the toxic loans that the supply siders want. We have this from Marketwatch:

"Michele Bachmann, the Club for Growth, and others in the right-wing coalition have now made their agenda for the financial sector very clear: they yearn to return to the thrilling days of yesteryear, so the loan arrangers can ride again – untrammeled by any rules restraining irresponsibility, excess, deception, and most of all, infinite leverage," Frank said in a statement.

I have spent a lot of time here independently arriving at the same conclusion regarding Paul Ryan, Eric Cantor, and even the libertarians like Ron Paul. Libertarianism affords no protection from these greedy Republicans. Even Mike Huckabee calls the Club for Growth the club of greed. We all know he is no longer running for president.

The Club for Growth has instituted the RINO Watch. RINO means "Republican in name only". People who do not support their easy money agenda are on the RINO Watch.

I have written about the desire of Jamie Dimon to seek the complete repeal of Dodd-Frank. Sorkin reported that on Kudlow awhile back. The consistent financial view of Bachmann, Dimon, Cantor and his hedge fund buddies, Ryan and the other financial heavyweights is that Dodd-Frank stands in the way of predatory loans. Indeed, the consumer regulations were set up to educate consumers about the toxic aspect of easy money loans. But most Republicans just don't want borrowers to know! And the crack cocaine of securitization is also another reason these people want the Dodd-Frank law repealed. The IMF wants austerity so that growth will come from ponzi lending! The Volcker Rule is a major component of Dodd-Frank. It stopped the casino as it relates to housing loans. The financial community wants to abolish it as their greed knows no bounds.

A particularly odious aspect of this greed is that many of the people who want to start the casino also are the first to tell the borrower that it is immoral for him to walk away from the toxic loan that he got in the last housing bubble.

But the difference between the last housing bubble and the next one is that the banks want guarantees for the next one. It would not surprise me that once the banks get what they want from the right wingers in repeal, that they will abandon them once the need for a blanket government guarantee of loans is demanded.

After all, they abandoned Obama and the Democrats once they got what they wanted out of them. Now they are floating articles about how Obama hates Wall Street and about how Barney Frank passes gas and how the S & P didn't attack the Tea Party.

And no, Maria Bartiromo, Jamie Dimon is not a rock star. Rock stars usually don't advocate hurtful loans, although I suppose we could ask Ted Nugent if he supports the predatory lenders.

We need serious infrastructure projects. **Certainly the jobs program of these Republicans: ponzi, hurtful, toxic loans, can't be the only solution.**

Helpful Links:

http://blogs.marketwatch.com/election/2011/01/06/gops-bachmann-seeks-to-repeal-dodd-frankcompletely

http://www.rightwingwatch.org/content/club-growth

http://en.wikipedia.org/wiki/Club_for_Growth

Top 10 Reasons Why I Won't Vote Republican Ever Again

My top 10 reasons for never wanting to vote for a Republican in my lifetime:

1. The CIA knew about the 911 hijackers before the hijackings, and covered it up according to former Counter Terrorism Czar Richard Clarke. I personally believe the CIA covered it up because the CIA was involved in 911. Why else would they cover it up? If they weren't involved they should have admitted the contact. I bet the CIA knew they were in the country taking flying lessons. It would be weird if they knew of the hijackers and yet failed to monitor them! Yeah right. The 911 Truthers are starting to look less tin foolish daily. And if they are right how could anyone vote Republican ever again?

2. Michele Bachmann, Rick Perry and Sarah Palin are Dominionists. But even traditional Christian doctrine teaches that Christ's kingdom was not of this world. In ignoring this basic teaching, the Dominionists believe that the sword or in modern times, tanks, nukes or whatever, should be used to take over the world by force for God. More weird religious positions are making it to the Republican mainstream. Even Newt Gingrich acknowledged that the Puritan leader, Oliver Cromwell, was a hero of his. Of course, Cromwell put the king of England to death in order to substitute one state religion for another. I guess that is right up Gingrich's alley! Not all Republican candidates lean toward Dominionism, but it sure seems like the number is increasing. We long for real Republicans, like Dwight

Eisenhower, who warned against extremists wanting to take away unemployment and social security. He also warned against the military-industrial complex. That is now renamed the military-industrial-financial complex. Ike knew about war more than anyone did. But he knew that the dark side of war was war profiteering.

3. The Republicans were taken over by the neocons, and all sorts of bad things happened, including number 1. But the most disturbing thing were the hundreds of thousands of people killed for oil wars. Big oil invited the Taliban to Texas in 1997 according to the BBC. The motive for involvement in the middle east was that these people rejected the pipeline to Halliburton investments in the Caspian Sea.The neocons want world domination, and are always pushing for an enemy. They are always pushing for a way to reflect blame off bankers and our greedy capitalism for our problems and place that blame on other nations. Other nations are not blameless, but that does not make them enemies.

4. The Republicans divert attention from real issues, like economic issues, to personal issues. They are always pushing the envelope regarding the separation of church and state. The Apostle Paul, from traditional Christian teaching, always viewed state religion as being false religion. The Terry Schiavo debacle was one example of butting in to the private affairs of citizens. Will private citizens make mistakes? Sure. But is the tradeoff being subjected to state religion worth it? Religious history shows the mess created by the fusion of church and state.

5. The Republicans want the repeal of Dodd-Frank. Clearly the reason is that they want massive ponzi, toxic loans against main street in the future. There is no other valid reason for the repeal of Dodd-

Frank in it's entirety, which is what Michele Bachmann, Eric Cantor, and many bankers want. Yes, both parties were up to their eyeballs in the first housing bubble. But Dodd-Frank is an effort by the Democrats to rein in the casino. The lies of Fox News pundits continues, as clearly the housing bubble would have been contained had it ended in mid 2003. Fox diverts from the private banking that took over after mid 2003. That was when the CRA pulled out of the process, and, as House of Cards said, the private shadow banking took over. Andrew Napolitano just last night said that the CRA and the community reinvestment act, which only resulted in about 24 percent of subprime loans, was the housing bubble. His listeners on Fox have no clue that the unregulated Shadow banks were the reason the housing bubble went wild.

6. The lies of Fox News pundits continues, as clearly the housing bubble would have been contained had it ended in mid 2003. Fox diverts from the private banking that took over after mid 2003. That was when the CRA pulled out of the process, and, as House of Cards said, the private shadow banking took over. I repeat, Andrew Napolitano just last night said (and we are in August of 2011) that the CRA and the community reinvestment act, which only resulted in about 24 percent of subprime loans, was the housing bubble. His listeners on Fox have no clue that the unregulated Shadow banks were the reason the housing bubble went wild. The Republicans seek a repeal of Dodd-Frank based upon the lie that deregulation did nothing bad. A vote for Republicans is a vote for Fox News and for pundits who lie continually. And nothing hits at the foundation of democracy as continual lying. We aren't talking about the breaking of an occasional campaign promise here. We are talking about continual lying.

7. The mainstream press, not just Fox, is just not reporting the news. How many of you knew that the Taliban went to Texas in 1997 as shown by point 3 above? Why do we have to rely on the BBC to tell us what is going on in our own country? Why would this be covered up by our news? Well, it is pretty obvious that the link of the Taliban going to Texas with such understandings about the CIA knowing about the hijackers before hand would point to massive government criminality in the Bush/Cheney era. Once your company gets rejected for a needed pipeline to your oil investments, you have motive to do bad things. And that motive can be realized if you win the election in 2000 by questionable means.

8. The Republicans divide people into old versus young, main street versus poor, us versus them, white versus everyone else. The only real division that makes any sense, as to actual harm to main street, is bankers versus everyone else. CNBC and a giddy Melissa Frances makes Jamie Dimon out to be a hero. But we know that the bankers are not heroes. We know that the military-industrial-financial complex is not heroic if left unchecked by the failure of democracy to monitor and control the complex. If the complex gains complete control, in a world order controlled by irresponsible people we can have World War 3. We can have banker attacks on main street with toxic loans. And that attack is made even more odious as any consumer protection agency is stripped of power to even explain the toxicity of toxic loans. Yes, it is true. Bankers don't even want people to understand toxic loans because that will stop the next housing bubble.

When the Tea Party blames people for not understanding the toxic loans in the last housing bubble, it is dirty for them not to acknowledge that this is what the bankers want, no understanding of the loans you are taking out! The reason that the big banks versus main street division is valid is because the banking cabal is international. That mean it is an international cabal versus America when you get right down to it. Will Rogers identified this cabal in the Great Depression and even referred to them as being international in scope.

9. The new financial order has certainly swallowed up the Democrats as well, but at least they are trying to take the traditional Democratic line, in protecting the people through Dodd-Frank. The protection from bankers was a key educational advantage of having the Democrats in charge during the Great Depression of the last century. The reason not to vote Republican is because the Democrats are trying. That does not mean that they have not succumbed to the Republican ways. Certainly fighting the Republican oil wars has been a stain on the party. The pressure should be on for the wars to wind down. But you can't really see the Republicans without escalating wars can you? I have listened to Republican candidates fall over themselves to see which could be the most hawkish. We run the risk of World War 3 if we keep electing Republicans.

10. Republicans have lost their legitimacy to rule. At the point in which the Democrats become as bad as the Republicans, there will be no point in voting at all. That could happen at any time sorry to say. We just have to monitor the situation, and not just by mainstream media. And this would not be a reason to ever vote for a party that could have destroyed thousands of Americans just to make money on a pipeline to the Caspian Sea. I would like to see the Republicans go away as a political party because they have lost their legitimacy to rule. But since they control the media most Americans will never know it.

Article Links:

http://www.thedailybeast.com/articles/2011/08/11/september-11th-anniversary-richard-clarke-s-explosive-cia-cover-up-charge.html

http://news.bbc.co.uk/2/hi/world/west_asia/37021.stm

Summary:

I have taken heat for discussing Ron Paul, an almost untouchable figure to his supporters. I like Ron Paul. I respect Dr Paul as a thinker. But I also understand that his views add to the bad behavior of the Dirty Republicans who may be using him. Add to that, while he is not an anarchist, albeit perhaps a peaceful one, some of his followers are revolutionary anarchists, especially if you listen to what they say. Freedom without responsibility for disadvantaged and elderly has anarchist tendencies. And certainly his views regarding the borrowers who were fooled by lenders is not correct. Borrowers were like victims of a large ponzi scheme. Yet Ron Paul does not realize that in his efforts to gain supporters in the Tea Party from his Libertarian foundation.

While the Republicans are getting it from all directions in the comment sections on most websites, expect to see easy money toxic loans before 2020. Americans must educate themselves if they are not to be victims of a massive transfer of wealth from the middle class to the banker class. It is clear that the banks want borrowers to be in the dark and dumb. They make more money that way. They did it before and they want to do it again. And this time, unlike in the days of Will Rogers, the media undermines the middle class and all borrowers.

Hopefully my books and ebooks will cause people to share word of mouth the need to reject all toxic mortgages from now on. I support the 30 year mortgage, but a fixed one with a large down payment. But even those can be risky when bankers want to blow more housing bubbles with their hedge fund buddies! The bankers are seeking to limit the power of the new consumer protection agency, because they want ever more obscurity regarding their loans. The nature of the ponzi last decade is that it was premeditated. And the banks now want to do three more things to increase their likelihood of a new housing bubble. 1. They want to skirt capital requirements by their relationships to hedge funds. 2. They want to allow hedge funds to get rid of the too big to fail stigma, so that these hedge funds can help the banks skirt the capital requirements. That would require the weakening of the Dodd-Frank Act. 3. The most insidious thing the big banks want to do is to limit the ability of the poor to understand what kind of loans they are getting.

Our work is to warn our friends and others about this impending housing bubble, which most likely will be blown before 2020. Apparently that is the Republican jobs program, an attack on those unsuspecting with an eye toward enslaving them with bad loans. This is just dirty, dirty business on the part of the Tea Party/Hedge Fund alliance. I support an end to QE, which causes speculation among the wealthy, and I support a massive jobs program based on our infrastructure needs. But I hold out hope that our government will protect America from a new housing bubble. Certainly many Republicans and quite a few Democrats want predatory lending to return. I just think that is dangerous and hurtful to our nation.

I want to touch upon the recent debt ceiling debate of 2011, and the media response. It appears the media is owned by the hedge funds in some very sinister way. While the Republicans are getting it from all directions on every website except the really conservative ones the articles are not singling out the Tea Party in the way the S & P did when they spoke of the downgrade. Here is the deal, the S & P cited brinkmanship on the part of the Tea Party, without mentioning them by name as a reason for the downgrade. It was obvious who caused the brinkmanship. Remember the IMF balanced budget they tried to push through here like in Italy?

And the Tea Party also didn't want to go for the shared sacrifice of taxes and cuts and the S & P called them out, not by name, on that as well. Too many articles about Obama and too few articles about the Tea Party in all of this. This of course affirms the truth that the bankers control the media, and that we no longer have a free mainstream press even though we have free speech in the USA. Remember to trust your own thinking and not that of the mainstream media going forward.

About the Author

Gary Anderson grew up in California and developed an interest in real estate during the Orange County boom of the 70's. He rekindled that interest in Nevada at the top of the boom, when inventories were building to dangerous levels, in mid-2005.

Since then he has striven to figure out the root causes of the real estate bubble and has contributed to major financial websites like Seeking Alpha and Business Insider. Mr. Anderson gives a muckraking appraisal of the financial system but is determined to avoid divisions over ethnicity. His books will reflect a fairness to all because all were victimized by the behavior of a few.

In the author's opinion, books and ebooks written by those who try to unravel the murky behavior of the big bankers are important. Without these studies it will be difficult for the nation to distance itself from the will of predatory bankers. The author supports Occupy Wall Street as long as the movement remains peaceful and dedicated to uncovering bad banking behavior.

The mainstream media will not allow for a massive revelation of who is to blame for the housing crisis, and what those to blame will do in the future. The populace has a general understanding that something was done incorrectly, but is largely unaware of the predatory nature of the international banking system.

The mainstream news media has distorted the facts regarding the cause of the housing bubble, and these books prove that the course of events was actually much different than stories that were misleading, polluting our popular beliefs. Based on that foundation it is easy to see who wants more housing bubbles, and how they will be able to pull it off in the midst of economic predictions of slow economic growth.

The banks have a plan, and it will cause more financial misery for our young and old going forward. The timeline is known only to the bankers, but they plan night and day for the time that they can write loans that they are not responsible for maintaining. House values will be manipulated going forward, just as speculation drives gasoline and food prices beyond their intrinsic worth.